Central Schemes for Multi-Dimensional Hamilton-Jacobi Equations

NASA Technical Reports Server (NTRS)

The BiblioGov Project is an effort to expand awareness of the public documents and records of the U.S. Government via print publications. In broadening the public understanding of government and its work, an enlightened democracy can grow and prosper. Ranging from historic Congressional Bills to the most recent Budget of the United States Government, the BiblioGov Project spans a wealth of government information. These works are now made available through an environmentally friendly, print-on-demand basis, using only what is necessary to meet the required demands of an interested public. We invite you to learn of the records of the U.S. Government, heightening the knowledge and debate that can lead from such publications.

Included are the following Collections:

Budget of The United States Government
Presidential Documents
United States Code
Education Reports from ERIC
GAO Reports
History of Bills
House Rules and Manual
Public and Private Laws

Code of Federal Regulations
Congressional Documents
Economic Indicators
Federal Register
Government Manuals
House Journal
Privacy act Issuances
Statutes at Large

Central Schemes for Multi-Dimensional Hamilton-Jacobi Equations

Steve Bryson[*]   Doron Levy[†]

August 23, 2001

Abstract

We present new, efficient central schemes for multi-dimensional Hamilton-Jacobi equations. These non-oscillatory, non-staggered schemes are first- and second-order accurate and are designed to scale well with an increasing dimension. Efficiency is obtained by carefully choosing the location of the evolution points and by using a one-dimensional projection step. First- and second-order accuracy is verified for a variety of multi-dimensional, convex and non-convex problems.

Key words. Hamilton-Jacobi equations, central schemes, high resolution.

AMS(MOS) subject classification. Primary 65M06; secondary 35L99.

1 Introduction

In this work we consider numerical approximations for solutions of multi-dimensional Hamilton-Jacobi (HJ) equations of the form

$$\frac{\partial \phi(\vec{x}, t)}{\partial t} + H(\vec{x}, \phi, \nabla \phi) = 0, \qquad \vec{x} \in \mathbb{R}^N, \tag{1.1}$$

subject to the initial data $\phi(\vec{x}, t=0) = \phi_0(\vec{x})$.

Hamilton-Jacobi equations are of special interest in a variety of applications, such as, *e.g.*, optimal control theory, image processing, geometric optics, differential games and the calculus of variations. When the Hamiltonian does not depend on ϕ, solutions for (1.1) with smooth initial data will typically remain continuous but will develop discontinuous derivatives in finite time. Such solutions are not unique, and therefore

---

[*]Program in Scientific Computing/Computational Mathematics, Stanford University and the NASA Advanced Supercomputing Division, NASA Ames Research Center, Moffett Field, CA 94035-1000; bryson@nas.nasa.gov

[†]Department of Mathematics, Stanford University, Stanford, CA 94305-2125; dlevy@math.stanford.edu

a mechanism is required for singling out a "physically relevant solution", the *viscosity solution*. For convex Hamiltonians the viscosity solution coincides with the limit solution obtained by the vanishing viscosity method [11]. Extensions to general Hamiltonians were introduced by Crandall and Lions in [7], and have been systematically studied thereafter in a series of works [3, 5, 6, 25].

Hamilton-Jacobi equations are closely related to hyperbolic conservation laws. Yet while the literature on numerical methods for conservation laws is flourishing, very little attention is given to numerical methods for HJ equations. This is surprising given their increasing role in different applications. Crandall and Lions introduced in [8] first-order numerical approximations to the viscosity solution of a simplified version of (1.1), with a Hamiltonian that only depends on the derivative of ϕ. Discontinuous Galerkin (DG) methods for HJ equations were introduced in [10, 22]. Multi-dimensional DG schemes are based on transforming a scalar equation into a weakly hyperbolic system which is over- or under-determined, hence an additional least-squares step is required to single out a solution. High-order Godunov-type methods were introduced in Shu [32, 33], and were based on an Essentially Non-Oscillatory (ENO) reconstruction step that was evolved in time with a first-order monotone flux. The least dissipative flux, the Godunov flux, requires solving Riemann problems at cell interfaces. Central schemes avoid these difficulties by evolving the solution in smooth regions, i.e., by averaging over discontinuities. Such schemes have been widely studied for conservation laws, the prototype being the first-order Lax-Friedrichs (LxF) scheme [9]. A one-dimensional second-order extension is due to Nessyahu and Tadmor [31]. Central schemes do not require Riemann solvers, which makes them suitable for solving systems of equations and for multi-dimensional problems. Extensions to two-space dimensions were done in [2, 14]; high-order central schemes were developed in [4, 23, 24, 28]; semi-discrete schemes that reduced the numerical dissipation and eliminated the staggering were developed in [16, 17, 19].

Central schemes have recently been extended to the HJ equations in [30], which applied the first- and second-order staggered central schemes of [14, 31] to HJ equations in one and two space dimensions. L^1 convergence of order one for this scheme was proved in [29]. In [18], a second-order semi-discrete scheme was presented, following the techniques for hyperbolic conservation laws [16, 19]. While less dissipative, this scheme requires the estimation of the local speed of propagation, which is computationally intensive in particular in multi-dimensional problems. In a later work, [17], the numerical viscosity was further reduced by computing more precise information about local speed of propagation.

In this paper we derive non-staggered fully-discrete central schemes for approximating solutions of (1.1). These methods combine the ideas of [18, 30], with several additional ingredients. Our scheme is presented as an N-dimensional algorithm which is designed with special consideration to performance and scaling to higher dimensions. We develop both first- and second-order accurate schemes. These schemes are based on a projection step which is one-dimensional regardless of the dimension of the problem. The methods described in this paper can also be thought of as the first step toward higher-order schemes, which is the subject of a forthcoming paper.

This paper is organized as follows: In Section 2 we develop our first and second order scheme in one dimension. Section 3 is the heart of the paper, where we generalize these schemes to N dimensions, first introducing a multi-index notation, then deriving the location of the evolution points, and finally presenting the algorithm. Section 4 presents various examples, demonstrating the first- and second-order convergence of these schemes. We present a sample code implementation of our 2D second-order algorithm in the appendix.

Acknowledgment: We would like to thank Ian Mitchell for helpful discussions and for suggesting the averaging strategy that is used to avoid staggering in the schemes. We also thank Volker Elling for helpful comments on early drafts of this paper.

2 The One-Dimensional Scheme

Consider the one dimensional Hamilton-Jacobi (HJ) equation

$$\phi_t + H\left(\phi_x\right) = 0, \tag{2.1}$$

subject to the initial data $\phi(x, t\!=\!0) = \phi_0(x)$. In order to approximate solutions of (2.1) we introduce a grid in space and time with mesh spacings, Δx and Δt, respectively. We denote the grid points by $x_i = i\Delta x$ and $t^n = n\Delta t$, and the fixed mesh ratio by $\lambda = \Delta t/\Delta x$. Let φ_i^n denote the approximate value of $\phi(x_i, t^n)$, and $(\varphi_x)_i^n$ denote the approximate value of the derivative $\phi_x(x_i, t^n)$. We define $(\Delta\varphi)_{i+\frac{1}{2}}^n := \varphi_{i+1}^n - \varphi_i^n$.

Given φ_i^n, an approximate solution at time t^n, the approximate solution at the next time step t^{n+1}, φ_i^{n+1}, is obtained as follows:

1. *Reconstruct* a continuous piecewise-polynomial from the data, φ_i^n, and sample it at the half-integer points, $\{x_{i+1/2}\}$, to obtain the values of $\varphi_{i+\frac{1}{2}}^n$ and its derivative, $(\varphi_x)_i^n$. The order of the polynomial is related to the overall order of accuracy of the method.

2. *Evolve* $\varphi_{i+\frac{1}{2}}^n$ by solving (2.1) from time t^n to time t^{n+1}, obtaining $\varphi_{i+\frac{1}{2}}^{n+1}$. This evolution is done at the half-integer grid points where the reconstruction is smooth, so long as the CFL condition $\lambda\left|H'\left(\varphi_x\right)\right| \le 1/2$ is satisfied.

3. *Project* $\varphi_{i+\frac{1}{2}}^{n+1}$ back onto the integer grid points $\{x_i\}$ to get φ_i^{n+1}.

2.1 A First Order Method

The derivation of the first-order method starts by reconstructing a piecewise-linear interpolant of the form

$$\varphi\left(x, t^n\right) := \sum_i \left[\varphi_i^n + \frac{(\Delta\varphi)_{i+\frac{1}{2}}^n}{\Delta x}\left(x - x_i\right)\right]\chi_{i+\frac{1}{2}}(x), \tag{2.2}$$

where $\chi_{i+\frac{1}{2}}(x)$ is the characteristic function of the interval $[x_i, x_{i+1})$. The values of the interpolant (2.2) and its derivative at the half-integer grid points, $x_{i\pm\frac{1}{2}}$ are

$$\varphi^n_{i\pm\frac{1}{2}} = \varphi^n_i \pm \frac{1}{2}(\Delta\varphi)^n_{i\pm\frac{1}{2}}, \qquad (\varphi_x)^n_{i\pm\frac{1}{2}} = \frac{(\Delta\varphi)^n_{i\pm\frac{1}{2}}}{\Delta x}.$$

Integrating (2.1) in time from t^n to t^{n+1} at $x_{i\pm\frac{1}{2}}$ gives

$$\varphi^{n+1}_{i\pm\frac{1}{2}} = \varphi^n_{i\pm\frac{1}{2}} - \Delta t H\left((\varphi_x)^n_{i\pm\frac{1}{2}}\right) = \varphi^n_i \pm \frac{1}{2}(\Delta\varphi)^n_{i\pm\frac{1}{2}} - \Delta t H\left((\varphi_x)^n_{i\pm\frac{1}{2}}\right).$$

Finally, we project the evolved solution back onto the original grid points. For a first-order method it is sufficient to average $\varphi^{n+1}_{i\pm 1/2}$,

$$\begin{aligned}
\varphi^{n+1}_i &= \frac{\varphi^{n+1}_{i+\frac{1}{2}} + \varphi^{n+1}_{i-\frac{1}{2}}}{2} = \\
&= \varphi^n_i + \frac{1}{4}\left((\Delta\varphi)^n_{i+\frac{1}{2}} - (\Delta\varphi)^n_{i-\frac{1}{2}}\right) - \frac{\Delta t}{2}\left[H\left(\frac{(\Delta\varphi)^n_{i+\frac{1}{2}}}{\Delta x}\right) + H\left(\frac{(\Delta\varphi)^n_{i-\frac{1}{2}}}{\Delta x}\right)\right].
\end{aligned} \qquad (2.3)$$

The intermediate values $\varphi^{n+1}_{i\pm 1/2}$ are the same as those computed in the first-order method in [31], so in one dimension we only add the projection step. This eliminates the grid staggering in [31] with little computational cost since no additional flux evaluations are required.

2.2   A Second Order Method

The second-order scheme is based on a piecewise-quadratic interpolant of the form

$$\varphi(x, t^n) := \sum_i \left[\varphi^n_i + \frac{(\Delta\varphi)^n_{i+\frac{1}{2}}}{\Delta x}(x - x_i) + \frac{1}{2}\frac{\mathcal{D}(\Delta\varphi)^n_{i+\frac{1}{2}}}{(\Delta x)^2}(x - x_i)(x - x_{i+1})\right]\chi_{i+\frac{1}{2}}. \quad (2.4)$$

Here, $\mathcal{D}$ is a limiter whose goal is to prevent oscillations while maintaining the order of accuracy of the method. There are various possibilities for choosing such limiters (see [37]). One such example is the Min-Mod limiter,

$$\mathcal{D}f_i := \mathrm{MM}\left[\theta(f_{i+1} - f_i), \frac{1}{2}(f_{i+1} - f_{i-1}), \theta(f_{i+1} - f_i)\right], \qquad 1 \le \theta \le 2,$$

where the Min-Mod function is defined as

$$\mathrm{MM}(x_1, x_2, \ldots) := \begin{cases} \min_j\{x_j\}, & \text{if all } x_j > 0, \\ \max_j\{x_j\}, & \text{if all } x_j < 0, \\ 0, & \text{otherwise.} \end{cases}$$

Since the solution of the HJ equations generally has a discontinuous first-derivative, we follow [18] by limiting the second-derivative. With the Min-Mod limiter, the second derivative is approximated by $\mathcal{D}(\Delta\varphi)^n_{i+1/2}/(\Delta x)^2$, where

$$\begin{aligned}
\mathcal{D}(\Delta\varphi)^n_{i+\frac{1}{2}} = \mathrm{MM}\Big[&\theta\left((\Delta\varphi)^n_{i+\frac{3}{2}} - (\Delta\varphi)^n_{i+\frac{1}{2}}\right), \frac{1}{2}\left((\Delta\varphi)^n_{i+\frac{3}{2}} - (\Delta\varphi)^n_{i-\frac{1}{2}}\right), \\
&\theta\left((\Delta\varphi)^n_{i+\frac{1}{2}} - (\Delta\varphi)^n_{i-\frac{1}{2}}\right)\Big].
\end{aligned}$$

Sampling (2.4) and its derivative at the half-integer grid points gives

$$\varphi_{i\pm\frac{1}{2}}^n = \varphi_i^n \pm \frac{1}{2}(\Delta\varphi)_{i\pm\frac{1}{2}}^n - \frac{1}{8}\mathcal{D}(\Delta\varphi)_{i\pm\frac{1}{2}}^n, \qquad (\varphi_x)_{i\pm\frac{1}{2}}^n = \frac{(\Delta\varphi)_{i\pm\frac{1}{2}}^n}{\Delta x}.$$

We integrate (2.1) from time t^n to time t^{n+1} using the second-order midpoint quadrature

$$\int_{t^n}^{t^{n+1}} H\left(\varphi_x\left(x_{i\pm\frac{1}{2}}, t^n\right)\right) dt \approx \Delta t H\left((\varphi_x)_{i\pm\frac{1}{2}}^{n+\frac{1}{2}}\right).$$

The required mid-values, $\varphi_x\left(x_{i\pm\frac{1}{2}}, t^{n+\frac{1}{2}}\right)$, can be predicted using a Taylor expansion,

$$\varphi_x\left(x_{i\pm\frac{1}{2}}, t^{n+\frac{1}{2}}\right) = \varphi_x\left(x_{i\pm\frac{1}{2}}, t^n\right) + \frac{1}{2}\Delta t \varphi_{tx}\left(x_{i\pm\frac{1}{2}}, t^n\right) + O\left((\Delta t)^2\right) =$$

$$= \varphi_x\left(x_{i\pm\frac{1}{2}}, t^n\right) - \frac{1}{2}\Delta t H'\left(\varphi_x\left(x_{i\pm\frac{1}{2}}, t^n\right)\right)\varphi_{xx}\left(x_{i\pm\frac{1}{2}}, t^n\right) + O\left((\Delta t)^2\right) \approx$$

$$\approx \frac{(\Delta\varphi)_{i\pm\frac{1}{2}}^n}{\Delta x} - \frac{1}{2}\lambda H'\left(\frac{(\Delta\varphi)_{i\pm\frac{1}{2}}^n}{\Delta x}\right)\frac{\mathcal{D}(\Delta\varphi)_{i\pm\frac{1}{2}}^n}{\Delta x},$$

which leads to

$$\varphi_{i\pm\frac{1}{2}}^{n+1} = \varphi_{i\pm\frac{1}{2}}^n - \Delta t H\left(\frac{(\Delta\varphi)_{i\pm\frac{1}{2}}^n}{\Delta x} - \frac{1}{2}\lambda H'\left(\frac{(\Delta\varphi)_{i\pm\frac{1}{2}}^n}{\Delta x}\right)\frac{\mathcal{D}(\Delta\varphi)_{i\pm\frac{1}{2}}^n}{\Delta x}\right). \qquad (2.5)$$

Finally, we project (2.5) back onto the integer grid points using a quadratic interpolant

$$\begin{aligned}
\varphi_i^{n+1} &= \varphi_{i-\frac{1}{2}}^{n+1} + \frac{(\Delta\varphi)_i^{n+1}}{\Delta x}\left(x_i - x_{i-\frac{1}{2}}\right) + \frac{1}{2}\frac{\mathcal{D}(\Delta\varphi)_i^{n+1}}{(\Delta x)^2}\left(x_i - x_{i-\frac{1}{2}}\right)\left(x_i - x_{i+\frac{1}{2}}\right) = \\
&= \varphi_{i-\frac{1}{2}}^{n+1} + \frac{1}{2}(\Delta\varphi)_i^{n+1} - \frac{1}{8}\mathcal{D}(\Delta\varphi)_i^{n+1},
\end{aligned}$$

where $(\Delta\varphi)_i^{n+1} = \varphi_{i+\frac{1}{2}}^{n+1} - \varphi_{i-\frac{1}{2}}^{n+1}$, and

$$\begin{aligned}
\mathcal{D}(\Delta\varphi)_i^{n+1} &= \text{MM}\Big[\theta\left((\Delta\varphi)_{i+1}^{n+1} - (\Delta\varphi)_i^{n+1}\right), \frac{1}{2}\left((\Delta\varphi)_{i+1}^{n+1} - (\Delta\varphi)_{i-1}^{n+1}\right), \\
&\qquad \theta\left((\Delta\varphi)_i^{n+1} - (\Delta\varphi)_{i-1}^{n+1}\right)\Big].
\end{aligned}$$

Remark. We would like to note that even in the 1D scheme, there are several differences between our method and the second-order scheme in [30]. A second-order interpolant is used to re-project the evolved fields back onto the original grid points, resulting with a non-staggered grid compared with the staggered scheme in [30]. Also, we follow [18] by applying the nonlinear slope limiters to the second derivative.

3   Generalization to N Dimensions

We are concerned with approximating solutions of the N-dimensional HJ equation of the form

$$\phi_t + H(\nabla\phi) = 0, \qquad \vec{x} \in \mathbb{R}^N, \tag{3.1}$$

subject to the initial data $\phi(\vec{x}, t) = \phi_0(\vec{x})$.

In Section 3.1 we introduce a multi-index notation, which allows a presentation that nicely parallels the one-dimensional case. We then compute the optimal location of the evolution points. Sections 3.2 and 3.3 develop the first- and second-order N-dimensional schemes. The first-order method in §3.2 below applies as is to the case where the Hamiltonian H depends also on $\vec{x}$ and ϕ. We extend the second-order method of §3.3 to this more general case in a remark.

3.1   Preliminaries

A multi-index notation. We define the multi-index $\alpha = (\alpha_1, \alpha_2, \ldots, \alpha_N)$, and denote by x_α, the point $x_\alpha = \left(x_{\alpha_1}^{(1)}, x_{\alpha_2}^{(2)}, \ldots, x_{\alpha_N}^{(N)} \right) \in \mathbb{R}^N$. Here $x^{(k)}$ denotes the k-th coordinate of x so $x_{\alpha_k}^{(k)} = \alpha_k \Delta x^{(k)}$. For example, in the conventional three-dimensional notation with indices i, j and k and components (x, y, z), $\alpha = (i, j, k)$ and $x_\alpha = (x_i, y_j, z_k)$.

For a given α we define the special multi-indices $\alpha \pm e_k := (\alpha_1, \ldots, \alpha_k \pm 1, \ldots, \alpha_N)$, which denotes an increment in the k direction. Then $\varphi_\alpha^n = \varphi(x_{\alpha_1}^{(1)}, x_{\alpha_2}^{(2)}, \ldots, x_{\alpha_N}^{(N)}; t^n)$ and $\varphi_{\alpha \pm e_k}^n = \varphi(x_{\alpha_1}^{(1)}, \ldots, x_{\alpha_k}^{(k)} \pm \Delta x^{(k)}, \ldots, x_{\alpha_N}^{(N)}; t^n)$. Finally, we denote the evolution points with the multi-indices $\pm := (\alpha_1 \pm a, \alpha_2 \pm a, \ldots, \alpha_N \pm a)$, for some constant a, so that $\varphi_\pm^n = \varphi(x_{\alpha_1}^{(1)} \pm a\Delta x^{(1)}, x_{\alpha_2}^{(2)} \pm a\Delta x^{(2)}, \ldots, x_{\alpha_N}^{(N)} \pm a\Delta x^{(N)}; t^n)$.

The location of the evolution points. We would like to determine the optimal location of the evolution points. For simplicity we assume a grid point at the origin, $x = (0, 0, \ldots, 0)$, and scale the coordinates such that $\forall k, \Delta x^{(k)} = 1$. The two evolution points will then be located at $x_\pm = (\pm a, \pm a, \ldots, \pm a)$ for a constant a that is yet to be determined.

Consider the evolution point x_+, which is at a distance $\sqrt{N}a$ from the origin. The value of φ at this point will be based on a polynomial that is constructed inside the (hyper-) volume bounded by the coordinate planes and the (hyper-) plane $\sum_{i=1}^{N} x^{(i)} = 1$. There will be discontinuities in the first-derivative of the piecewise-polynomial interpolant $\varphi(x, t^n)$ along the sides of this hyper-volume. Since we evolve the solution in smooth regions, an optimal choice of the evolution points is at an equidistant location from these boundaries. The diagonal line $(s, s, \ldots, s)$ (for some parameter s) intersects the (hyper-)plane $\sum_{i=1}^{N} x^{(i)} = 1$ at $s = 1/N$, or at the point $x_p = \left(\frac{1}{N}, \frac{1}{N}, \ldots, \frac{1}{N} \right)$ which is at a distance $1/\sqrt{N}$ from the origin (see Figure 3.1).

The optimal choice is to require that the evolution points are equidistant from the coordinate planes and the intersection point x_p. The distance from x_+ to all the coordinate planes is a. The distance from x_+ to x_p is $1/\sqrt{N} - a\sqrt{N}$, therefore the requirement that x_+ be equidistant from the coordinate planes and x_p is

$$a = \frac{1}{N + \sqrt{N}}.$$

The evolution points in [30] were chosen as $a = 1/4$, which places them equidistant between the origin and the intersection point x_p. In N dimensions this choice generalizes to $a = (2N)^{-1}$. In our case, when $N = 2$, $a = (2 + \sqrt{2})^{-1} \approx 0.29$ which is about 15% larger than the choice $a = 1/4$. When $N = 3$, $a = (3 + \sqrt{3})^{-1} \approx 0.21$ which is about 30% larger than the choice $a = 1/6$. Thus the optimal choice of a will allow larger mesh ratios, leading to larger time steps and less dissipation.

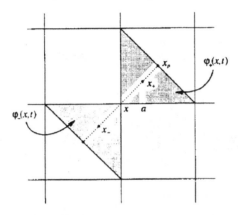

Figure 3.1: The location of the evolution points $x_\pm$ and x_p in 2D.

3.2 A First Order Method

For simplicity we assume that the spacing is identical in every direction, i.e., $\Delta x^{(k)} = \Delta x$, for all k. Generalization of the methods below to the case where $\Delta x^{(k)} \neq \Delta x^{(j)}$ for $k \neq j$ is straightforward. We define the forward- and backward-differences in the k-th component as $\Delta_k^+ \varphi_\alpha^n := \varphi_{\alpha+e_k}^n - \varphi_\alpha^n$ and $\Delta_k^- \varphi_\alpha^n := \varphi_\alpha^n - \varphi_{\alpha-e_k}^n$, respectively. At each grid point x_α we reconstruct two linear interpolants that are valid in the two hyper-quadrants that contain the points $x_\pm = x_\alpha \pm (a, \ldots, a)\Delta x$,

$$\varphi_\pm(x, t^n) := \varphi_\alpha^n + \sum_{k=1}^{N} \frac{\Delta_k^\pm \varphi_\alpha^n}{\Delta x} \left(x^{(k)} - x_{\alpha_k}^{(k)} \right). \tag{3.2}$$

In order to compute the solution at the next time step at x_α, we first compute the solution at time t^{n+1} at the evolution points $x_\pm$, and then average these two values. The value of the linear interpolant (3.2) at $x_\pm$ is

$$\varphi(x_\pm, t^n) = \varphi_\alpha^n \pm a \sum_{k=1}^{N} \Delta_k^\pm \varphi_\alpha^n,$$

and its derivative is

$$(\nabla\varphi)_{\pm}^n := \left(\frac{\Delta_1^{\pm}\varphi_{\alpha}^n}{\Delta x}, \ldots, \frac{\Delta_N^{\pm}\varphi_{\alpha}^n}{\Delta x} \right).$$

Hence, the values at the evolution points $x_{\pm}$ at the next time step, t^{n+1}, are given by

$$\varphi(x_{\pm}, t^{n+1}) = \varphi(x_{\pm}, t^n) - \int_{t^n}^{t^{n+1}} H\left(\nabla\varphi\left(x_{\pm}, t^n\right)\right) dt \approx \varphi(x_{\pm}, t^n) - \Delta t H\left((\nabla\varphi)_{\pm}^n\right) =$$

$$= \varphi_{\alpha}^n \pm a \sum_{k=1}^N \Delta_k^{\pm}\varphi_{\alpha}^n - \Delta t H\left(\frac{\Delta_1^{\pm}\varphi_{\alpha}^n}{\Delta x}, \ldots, \frac{\Delta_N^{\pm}\varphi_{\alpha}^n}{\Delta x}\right).$$

The value at t^{n+1} at x_{α} is finally obtained by averaging $\varphi_{\pm}^{n+1} := \varphi\left(x_{\pm}, t^{n+1}\right)$ (compare with (2.3)),

$$\begin{aligned} \varphi_{\alpha}^{n+1} &= \frac{1}{2}\left(\varphi_+^{n+1} + \varphi_-^{n+1}\right) = \hspace{4cm} (3.3)\\ &= \varphi_{\alpha}^n + \frac{a}{4}\left(\sum_{k=1}^N \Delta_k^+\varphi_{\alpha}^n - \sum_{k=1}^N \Delta_k^-\varphi_{\alpha}^n\right) - \\ &\quad - \frac{\Delta t}{2}\left(H\left(\frac{\Delta_1^+\varphi_{\alpha}^n}{\Delta x}, \ldots, \frac{\Delta_N^+\varphi_{\alpha}^n}{\Delta x}\right) + H\left(\frac{\Delta_1^-\varphi_{\alpha}^n}{\Delta x}, \ldots, \frac{\Delta_N^-\varphi_{\alpha}^n}{\Delta x}\right)\right). \end{aligned}$$

3.3 A Second Order Method

For simplicity we assume again that the mesh spacing is identical in every spatial direction, i.e., $\Delta x^{(k)} = \Delta x$, for all k. Similarly to the 1D case in Section 2.2, the N-dimensional second-order method is based on a piecewise-quadratic polynomial. For every grid node we reconstruct two N-dimensional quadratic interpolants: $\varphi_+(x, t^n)$ for the hyper-quadrant along the positive diagonal, and $\varphi_-(x, t^n)$ along the negative diagonal (see Figure 3.1),

$$\varphi_{\pm}(x, t^n) := \varphi_{\alpha}^n + \sum_{k=1}^N \frac{\Delta_k^{\pm}\varphi_0^n}{\Delta x}\left(x^{(k)} - x_{\alpha}^{(k)}\right) + \hspace{3cm} (3.4)$$

$$+ \frac{1}{2}\sum_{k=1}^N \frac{\mathcal{D}_k\Delta_k^{\pm}\varphi_{\alpha}^n}{(\Delta x)^2}\left(x^{(k)} - x_{\alpha}^{(k)}\right)\left(x^{(k)} - x_{\alpha\pm e_k}^{(k)}\right) +$$

$$+ \frac{1}{2}\sum_{j=1}^N \sum_{\substack{k=1 \\ k \neq j}}^N \frac{\mathcal{D}_j\Delta_k^{\pm}\varphi_{\alpha}^n}{(\Delta x)^2}\left(x^{(j)} - x_{\alpha}^{(j)}\right)\left(x^{(k)} - x_{\alpha}^{(k)}\right).$$

The Min-Mod limiter in the j-th direction acting on $\Delta_k^{\pm}\varphi_{\alpha}^n$ is

$$\begin{aligned} \mathcal{D}_j\Delta_k^{\pm}\varphi_{\alpha}^n = \text{MM}\Bigl[&\theta\left(\Delta_k^{\pm}\varphi_{\alpha+e_j}^n - \Delta_k^{\pm}\varphi_{\alpha}^n\right), \\ &\frac{1}{2}\left(\Delta_k^{\pm}\varphi_{\alpha+e_j}^n - \Delta_k^{\pm}\varphi_{\alpha-e_j}^n\right), \theta\left(\Delta_k^{\pm}\varphi_{\alpha}^n - \Delta_k^{\pm}\varphi_{\alpha-e_j}^n\right)\Bigr], \end{aligned}$$

so that $\mathcal{D}_j \Delta_k^\pm \varphi_\alpha^n / (\Delta x)^2$ approximates the second derivative $\partial^2 \varphi (x_\alpha, t^n) / \partial x^{(j)} \partial x^{(k)}$.

Now $x_\pm^{(k)} - x_\alpha^{(k)} = \pm a \Delta x$, $x_+^{(k)} - x_{\alpha+e_k}^{(k)} = (a-1) \Delta x$ and $x_-^{(k)} - x_{\alpha-e_k}^{(k)} = - (a-1) \Delta x$ so evaluating (3.4) at $x_\pm$

$$
\begin{aligned}
\varphi_\pm^n \quad &:= \quad \varphi_\pm (x_\pm, t^n) = \\
&= \quad \varphi_\alpha^n \pm a \sum_{k=1}^N \Delta_k^\pm \varphi_\alpha^n + \frac{a(a-1)}{2} \sum_{k=1}^N \mathcal{D}_k \Delta_k^\pm \varphi_\alpha^n + \frac{a^2}{2} \sum_{j=1}^N \sum_{\substack{k=1 \\ k \neq j}}^N \mathcal{D}_j \Delta_k^\pm \varphi_\alpha^n .
\end{aligned}
$$

The approximation to the first derivative of (3.4) in the p-th direction is given by

$$
\begin{aligned}
\frac{\partial \varphi_\pm (x, t^n)}{\partial x^{(p)}} &\approx \frac{\Delta_p^\pm \varphi_\alpha^n}{\Delta x} + \frac{\mathcal{D}_p \Delta_p^\pm \varphi_\alpha^n}{2 (\Delta x)^2} \left[\left(x_\pm^{(p)} - x_\alpha^{(p)} \right) + \left(x_\pm^{(p)} - x_{\alpha \pm e_p}^{(p)} \right) \right] + \\
&+ \frac{1}{2 (\Delta x)^2} \sum_{\substack{k=1 \\ k \neq p}}^N \left[\mathcal{D}_p \Delta_k^\pm \varphi_\alpha^n + \mathcal{D}_k \Delta_p^\pm \varphi_\alpha^n \right] \left(x_\pm^{(k)} - x_\alpha^{(k)} \right),
\end{aligned}
$$

which when evaluated at $x_\pm$ is

$$
\begin{aligned}
\left(\frac{\partial \varphi}{\partial x^{(p)}} \right)_\pm^n &:= \left. \frac{\partial \varphi_\pm (x, t^n)}{\partial x^{(p)}} \right|_{x_\pm} = \\
&= \frac{\Delta_p^\pm \varphi_\alpha^n}{\Delta x} \pm \frac{2a-1}{2} \frac{\mathcal{D}_p \Delta_p^\pm \varphi_\alpha^n}{\Delta x} \pm \frac{a}{2} \sum_{\substack{k=1 \\ k \neq p}}^N \frac{\mathcal{D}_p \Delta_k^\pm \varphi_\alpha^n + \mathcal{D}_k \Delta_p^\pm \varphi_\alpha^n}{\Delta x} .
\end{aligned}
$$

The approximation to the second derivative is given by

$$
\left(\frac{\partial^2 \varphi_\pm}{\partial x^{(q)} \partial x^{(p)}} \right)^n = \frac{\mathcal{D}_p \Delta_q^\pm \varphi_\alpha^n + \mathcal{D}_q \Delta_p^\pm \varphi_\alpha^n}{2 (\Delta x)^2} .
$$

The solution at the next time step at the evolution points $\varphi_\pm^{n+1}$ is obtained by evolving the reconstruction (3.4) according to (3.1). The integral of the Hamiltonian is approximated by a second-order midpoint quadrature, $\int_{t^n}^{t^{n+1}} H (\nabla \varphi (x_{i\pm}, t^n)) \, dt \approx \Delta t H \left((\nabla \varphi)_\pm^{n+\frac{1}{2}} \right)$, which at the evolution points gives

$$
\varphi_\pm^{n+1} = \varphi_\pm^n - \Delta t H \left((\nabla \varphi)_\pm^{n+\frac{1}{2}} \right). \tag{3.5}
$$

Here $(\nabla \varphi)_\pm^n := \left(\left(\frac{\partial \varphi}{\partial x^{(1)}} \right)_\pm^n, \ldots, \left(\frac{\partial \varphi}{\partial x^{(N)}} \right)_\pm^n \right)$ denotes the approximation to the gradient at $x_\pm$. The mid-values in time can be estimated via the Taylor expansion using (3.1),

$$
\begin{aligned}
\frac{\partial \varphi}{\partial x^{(p)}} \left(x_\pm, t^{n+\frac{1}{2}} \right) &= \frac{\partial \varphi}{\partial x^{(p)}} (x_\pm, t^n) + \frac{\Delta t}{2} \frac{\partial^2 \varphi}{\partial x^{(p)} \partial t} (x_\pm, t^n) + O (\Delta t^2) = \tag{3.6} \\
&= \frac{\partial \varphi}{\partial x^{(p)}} (x_\pm, t^n) - \frac{\Delta t}{2} \sum_{k=1}^N \frac{\partial}{\partial \frac{\partial \varphi}{\partial x^{(k)}}} H (\nabla \varphi (x_\pm, t^n)) \frac{\partial^2 \varphi}{\partial x^{(p)} \partial x^{(k)}} (x_\pm, t^n) + O (\Delta t^2) .
\end{aligned}
$$

Hence,

$$\left(\frac{\partial \varphi}{\partial x^{(p)}}\right)_{\pm}^{n+\frac{1}{2}} := \frac{\Delta_p^{\pm}\varphi_\alpha^n}{\Delta x} \pm \frac{2a-1}{2}\frac{\mathcal{D}_p\Delta_p^{\pm}\varphi_\alpha^n}{\Delta x} \pm \frac{a}{2}\sum_{\substack{k=1 \\ k\neq p}}^{N} \frac{\mathcal{D}_p\Delta_k^{\pm}\varphi_\alpha^n + \mathcal{D}_k\Delta_p^{\pm}\varphi_{0\alpha}^n}{\Delta x} -$$

$$-\frac{\Delta t}{2}\sum_{k=1}^{N}\frac{\partial}{\partial \frac{\partial \varphi}{\partial x^k}}H\left((\nabla\varphi)_{\pm}^n\right)\frac{\mathcal{D}_p\Delta_k^{\pm}\varphi_\alpha^n + \mathcal{D}_k\Delta_p^{\pm}\varphi_\alpha^n}{2\left(\Delta x\right)^2}.$$

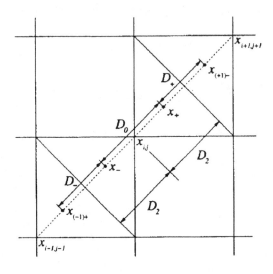

Figure 3.2: The location of the points x_+, x_-, $x_{(-1)+}$ and $x_{(+1)-}$ used in the projection step along with the distances D_0, D_+ and D_- in the two dimensional case.

All that remains is to project (3.5) back onto the original grid points, x_α. This projection is one-dimensional regardless of N. We use the four evolution points x_+, x_-,

$$x_{(-1)+} := \left(x_\alpha^{(1)} - \Delta x^{(1)} + a\Delta x^{(1)}, x_\alpha^{(2)} - \Delta x^{(2)} + a\Delta x^{(2)}, \ldots, x_\alpha^{(N)} - \Delta x^{(N)} + a\Delta x^{(N)}\right) \text{ and}$$

$$x_{(+1)-} := \left(x_\alpha^{(1)} + \Delta x^{(1)} - a\Delta x^{(1)}, x_\alpha^{(2)} + \Delta x^{(2)} - a\Delta x^{(2)}, \ldots, x_\alpha^{(N)} + \Delta x^{(N)} - a\Delta x^{(N)}\right) \text{ (see}$$

Figure 3.2). The distances between the evolution points are $D_0 := |x_+ - x_-| = 2a\sqrt{N}\Delta x$, $D_+ := |x_{(+1)-} - x_+| = (1-2a)\sqrt{N}\Delta x$, and $D_- := |x_{(-1)+} - x_-| = D_+$. We then define the approximations to the first derivative along the diagonal,

$$\frac{(d\varphi)_0^{n+1}}{D_0} := \frac{\varphi_+^{n+1} - \varphi_-^{n+1}}{D_0}, \qquad \frac{(d\varphi)_+^{n+1}}{D_+} := \frac{\varphi_{(+1)-}^{n+1} - \varphi_+^{n+1}}{D_+},$$

$$\frac{(d\varphi)_-^{n+1}}{D_-} := \frac{\varphi_+^{n+1} - \varphi_{(-1)+}^{n+1}}{D_-}.$$

The approximation to the second derivative is the limited difference $\mathcal{D}(d\varphi)_0^{n+1}/D_2$, where $D_2 = \frac{1}{2}(D_0 + D_+)$, and

$$
\mathcal{D}(d\varphi)_0^{n+1} = \text{MM}\left[\theta\left(\frac{(d\varphi)_+^{n+1}}{D_+} - \frac{(d\varphi)_0^{n+1}}{D_0}\right), \frac{1}{2}\left(\frac{(d\varphi)_+^{n+1}}{D_+} - \frac{(d\varphi)_-^{n+1}}{D_-}\right),\right.
$$
$$
\left. \theta\left(\frac{(d\varphi)_0^{n+1}}{D_0} - \frac{(d\varphi)_-^{n+1}}{D_-}\right)\right]. \tag{3.7}
$$

The approximated value at the next time step t^{n+1} at the grid point x_α is therefore given by

$$
\begin{aligned}
\varphi_\alpha^{n+1} &= \varphi_-^{n+1} + \frac{(d\varphi)_0^{n+1}}{D_0}(x_\alpha - x_-) + \frac{\mathcal{D}(d\varphi)_0^{n+1}}{2D_2}(x_\alpha - x_-)(x_\alpha - x_+) \\
&= \varphi_-^{n+1} + \frac{\varphi_+^{n+1} - \varphi_-^{n+1}}{D_0}\frac{D_0}{2} - \frac{\mathcal{D}(d\varphi)_0^{n+1}}{2D_2}\frac{D_0^2}{4} \\
&= \frac{1}{2}\left(\varphi_+^{n+1} + \varphi_-^{n+1}\right) - \frac{D_0^2}{8D_2}\mathcal{D}(d\varphi)_0^{n+1},
\end{aligned}
$$

where $\varphi_\pm^{n+1}$ is given by (3.5) and $\mathcal{D}(d\varphi)_0^{n+1}$ is given by (3.8).

Remarks.

1. If the Hamiltonian H depends also on $\bar{x}$ and ϕ, then (3.5) becomes

$$
\varphi_\pm^{n+1} = \varphi_\pm^n - \Delta t H\left(\bar{x}, \varphi_\pm^{n+\frac{1}{2}}, (\nabla\varphi)_\pm^{n+\frac{1}{2}}\right),
$$

where

$$
\varphi_\pm^{n+\frac{1}{2}} = \varphi_\pm^n - \frac{\Delta t}{2}H\left(\bar{x}, \varphi_\pm^n, (\nabla\varphi)_\pm^n\right),
$$

and the Taylor expansion (3.6) contains the additional term

$$
-\frac{\Delta t}{2}\left[\frac{\partial}{\partial x^{(p)}}H(\bar{x}, \varphi, \nabla\varphi) + \frac{\partial}{\partial\varphi}H(\bar{x}, \varphi, \nabla\varphi)\frac{\partial\varphi}{\partial x^{(p)}}\right]\Bigg|_{(x_\pm, t^n)}.
$$

2. We would like to stress that the fully-discrete scheme in [18] that was derived as an intermediate step in developing the semi-discrete scheme, was only first-order in time. Moreover, in 2D our scheme is based only on two flux evaluations compared with four flux evaluations in [17, 18]. It also does not require any estimation of the local speed of propagation at every grid point (as required in [17, 18]) at the price of being more dissipative.

We would like to summarize the second-order N-dimensional algorithm for a general Hamiltonian $H(\bar{x}, \phi, \nabla\phi)$:

Algorithm 3.1 *Let the distance of the evolution points from the origin be* $a = \frac{1}{N+\sqrt{N}}$.

1. *For each grid node x_α and each k compute*

$$\Delta_k^+ \varphi_\alpha^n = \varphi_{\alpha+e_k}^n - \varphi_\alpha^n \text{ and } \Delta_k^- \varphi_\alpha^n = \varphi_\alpha^n - \varphi_{\alpha-e_k}^n.$$

2. *For each grid node x_α and for each j and k compute*

$$\mathcal{D}_j \Delta_k^\pm \varphi_\alpha^n = \text{MM}\left[\theta\left(\Delta_k^\pm \varphi_{\alpha+e_j}^n - \Delta_k^\pm \varphi_\alpha^n\right), \frac{1}{2}\left(\Delta_k^\pm \varphi_{\alpha+e_j}^n - \Delta_k^\pm \varphi_{\alpha-e_j}^n\right),\right.$$
$$\left.\theta\left(\Delta_k^\pm \varphi_\alpha^n - \Delta_k^\pm \varphi_{\alpha-e_j}^n\right)\right].$$

3. *For each grid node x_α compute*

$$\varphi_\pm^n = \varphi_\alpha^n \pm a \sum_{k=1}^N \Delta_k^\pm \varphi_\alpha^n + \frac{a(a-1)}{2} \sum_{k=1}^N \mathcal{D}_k \Delta_k^\pm \varphi_\alpha^n + \frac{a^2}{2} \sum_{j=1}^N \sum_{\substack{k=1\\k\neq j}}^N \mathcal{D}_j \Delta_k^\pm \varphi_\alpha^n,$$

and for each p compute

$$\left(\frac{\partial\varphi}{\partial x^{(p)}}\right)_\pm^n = \frac{\Delta_p^\pm \varphi_\alpha^n}{\Delta x} \pm \frac{2a-1}{2} \frac{\mathcal{D}_p \Delta_p^\pm \varphi_\alpha^n}{\Delta x} \pm \frac{a}{2} \sum_{\substack{k=1\\k\neq p}}^N \frac{\mathcal{D}_p \Delta_k^\pm \varphi_\alpha^n + \mathcal{D}_k \Delta_p^\pm \varphi_\alpha^n}{\Delta x},$$

$$\left(\frac{\partial\varphi}{\partial x^{(p)}}\right)_\pm^{n+\frac{1}{2}} = \left(\frac{\partial\varphi}{\partial x^{(p)}}\right)_\pm^n - \frac{\Delta t}{2}\left[\frac{\partial}{\partial x^{(p)}} H\left(\vec{x}, \varphi_\pm^n, (\nabla\varphi)_\pm^n\right) + \right.$$
$$+ \frac{\partial}{\partial\varphi} H\left(\vec{x}, \varphi_\pm^n, (\nabla\varphi)_\pm^n\right)\left(\frac{\partial\varphi}{\partial x^{(p)}}\right)_\pm^n +$$
$$\left. + \sum_{k=1}^N \frac{\partial}{\partial \frac{\partial\varphi}{\partial x^k}} H\left(\vec{x}, \varphi_\pm^n, (\nabla\varphi)_\pm^n\right)\left[\frac{\mathcal{D}_p \Delta_k^\pm \varphi_\alpha^n + \mathcal{D}_k \Delta_p^\pm \varphi_\alpha^n}{2(\Delta x)^2}\right]\right],$$

$$\varphi_{\alpha\pm}^{n+1} = \varphi_\pm^n - \Delta t H\left((\nabla\varphi)_\pm^{n+\frac{1}{2}}\right),$$

where $H\left((\nabla\varphi)_\pm^n\right) = H\left(\left(\frac{\partial\varphi}{\partial x^{(1)}}\right)_\pm^n, \ldots, \left(\frac{\partial\varphi}{\partial x^{(N)}}\right)_\pm^n\right).$

4. *Let* $D_0 = 2a\sqrt{N}\Delta x$, $D_+ = D_- = (1-2a)\sqrt{N}\Delta x$. *For each x_α compute*

$$\frac{(d\varphi)_0^{n+1}}{D_0} = \frac{\varphi_{\alpha+}^{n+1} - \varphi_{\alpha-}^{n+1}}{D_0}, \frac{(d\varphi)_+^{n+1}}{D_+} = \frac{\varphi_{(\alpha+1)-}^{n+1} - \varphi_{\alpha+}^{n+1}}{D_+}, \frac{(d\varphi)_-^{n+1}}{D_-} = \frac{\varphi_{\alpha+}^{n+1} - \varphi_{(\alpha-1)+}^{n+1}}{D_-},$$

(where $\alpha \pm 1$ is the multi-index $(\alpha_1 \pm 1, \ldots, \alpha_N \pm 1)$)

$$\mathcal{D}\,(d\varphi)_0^{n+1} \;=\; \mathrm{MM}\left[\theta\left(\frac{(d\varphi)_+^{n+1}}{D_+} - \frac{(d\varphi)_0^{n+1}}{D_0}\right), \frac{1}{2}\left(\frac{(d\varphi)_+^{n+1}}{D_+} - \frac{(d\varphi)_-^{n+1}}{D_-}\right),\right.$$
$$\left.\theta\left(\frac{(d\varphi)_0^{n+1}}{D_0} - \frac{(d\varphi)_-^{n+1}}{D_-}\right)\right],$$

5. *For each x_α compute*

$$\varphi_\alpha^{n+1} = \frac{1}{2}\left(\varphi_{\alpha+}^{n+1} + \varphi_{\alpha-}^{n+1}\right) - \frac{D_0^2}{8D_2}\mathcal{D}\,(d\varphi)_0^{n+1}.$$

4   Numerical Examples

We demonstrate the schemes developed in Section 2 and Section 3 with several examples. Most of these examples are standard test cases that can be found, e.g., in [18, 30, 33].

Example 1: A convex Hamiltonian

We start by testing the performance of our schemes on a convex Hamiltonian. We approximate solutions of the one-dimensional equation

$$\phi_t + \frac{1}{2}\left(\phi_x + 1\right)^2 = 0, \tag{4.1}$$

subject to the initial data $\phi(x, 0) = -\cos(\pi x)$ and to periodic boundary conditions on $[0, 2]$. The change of variables, $u(x, t) = \phi_x(x, t) + 1$, transforms the equation into the Burger's equation, $u_t + \frac{1}{2}(u^2)_x = 0$, which can be solved via the method of characteristics [33]. As is well known, Burger's equation generally develops discontinuous solutions even with smooth initial data, and hence we expect the solutions of (4.1) to have discontinuous derivatives. In our case, the solution develops a singularity at time $t = \pi^{-2}$.

The results of our simulations are shown in Figure 4.1 and Figure 4.2. The order of accuracy of these methods is determined from the L^1-norm of the error (see [29]). The results before the singularity, at $T = 0.8/\pi^2$, are given in Table 4.1, and after the singularity at $T = 1.5/\pi^2$ in Table 4.2.

In 2D we solve a similar problem

$$\phi_t + \frac{1}{2}\left(\phi_x + \phi_y + 1\right)^2 = 0, \tag{4.2}$$

which can be reduced to a one-dimensional problem via the coordinate transformation $\begin{pmatrix} \xi \\ \eta \end{pmatrix} = \frac{1}{2}\begin{pmatrix} 1 & 1 \\ 1 & -1 \end{pmatrix}\begin{pmatrix} x \\ y \end{pmatrix}$. The results of the second-order calculations for the initial data $\phi(x, y, 0) = -\cos(\pi(x+y)/2) = -\cos(\pi\xi)$ are shown in Figures 4.3–4.4. The convergence rates for the first- and second-order 2D schemes before and after the development of the singularity are shown in Tables 4.3–4.4.

N	First-order method		Second-order method	
	L^1-error	L^1-order	L^1-error	L^1-order
40	0.0342	–	6.14×10^{-3}	–
80	0.0172	1.00	1.53×10^{-3}	2.00
160	0.0082	1.06	3.62×10^{-4}	2.08
320	0.0040	1.03	8.77×10^{-5}	2.04

Table 4.1: L^1-errors for the 1D convex HJ problem (4.1) before the singularity formation. $T = 0.8/\pi^2$.

N	First-order method		Second-order method	
	L^1-error	L^1-order	L^1-error	L^1-order
40	0.0788	–	0.0110	–
80	0.0379	1.06	2.70×10^{-3}	2.03
160	0.0183	1.05	6.79×10^{-4}	1.99
320	0.0091	1.00	2.28×10^{-5}	1.57

Table 4.2: L^1-errors for the 1D convex HJ problem (4.1) after the formation of the singularity. $T = 1.5/\pi^2$.

N	First-order method		Second-order method	
	L^1-error	L^1-order	L^1-error	L^1-order
50	0.299819	–	0.0261816	–
100	0.144967	1.05	0.0061162	2.10
200	0.0712024	1.03	0.00146501	2.06

Table 4.3: L^1-errors for the 2D convex HJ problem (4.2) before the singularity formation. $T = 0.8/\pi^2$.

N	First-order method		Second-order method	
	L^1-error	L^1-order	L^1-error	L^1-order
50	0.44437	–	0.0356362	–
100	0.215055	1.05	0.0101615	1.81
200	0.104421	1.02	0.00237225	2.10

Table 4.4: L^1-errors for the 2D convex HJ problem (4.2) after the singularity formation. $T = 1.5/\pi^2$.

We proceed with a 3D generalization of (4.2),

$$\phi_t + \frac{1}{2}\left(\phi_x + \phi_y + \phi_z + 1\right)^2 = 0, \tag{4.3}$$

subject to the initial data $\phi(x, y, 0) = -\cos(\pi(x + y + z)/3)$. The convergence results for the first- and second-order 3D schemes before and after the singularity formation are given in Tables 4.5–4.6.

N	First-order method		Second-order method	
	L^1-error	L^1-order	L^1-error	L^1-order
50	5.932	–	0.672	–
100	2.838	1.06	0.155	2.12
200	1.76	0.69	0.041	1.92

Table 4.5: L^1-errors for the 3D convex HJ problem (4.3) before the singularity formation. $T = 0.08$.

N	First-order method		Second-order method	
	L^1-error	L^1-order	L^1-error	L^1-order
50	8.801	–	0.776	–
100	4.148	1.09	0.171	2.18
200	2.138	0.96	0.055	1.65

Table 4.6: L^1-errors for the 3D convex HJ problem (4.3) after the singularity formation. $T = 0.152$.

Example 2: A non-convex Hamiltonian

In this example we deal with non-convex Hamilton-Jacobi equations. In 1D we solve

$$\phi_t - \cos(\phi_x + 1) = 0, \tag{4.4}$$

subject to the initial data, $\phi(x, 0) = -\cos(\pi x)$, and periodic boundary conditions on $[0, 2]$. In this case, (4.4), has a smooth solution for $t \lesssim 1.049/\pi^2$, after which a singularity forms. A second singularity forms at $t \approx 1.29/\pi^2$. The results are shown in Figures 4.5–4.6. The convergence results before and after the singularity formation are given in Tables 4.7–4.8.

In 2D we solve

$$\phi_t - \cos(\phi_x + \phi_y + 1) = 0, \tag{4.5}$$

subject to the initial data, $\phi(x, y, 0) = -\cos(\pi(x + y)/2)$, and periodic boundary conditions. The results are shown in Figures 4.7–4.8. The convergence results for the first-

N	First-order method		Second-order method	
	L^1-error	L^1-order	L^1-error	L^1-order
40	0.0406	–	7.71×10^{-3}	–
80	0.0206	0.99	2.00×10^{-3}	1.95
160	0.0099	1.06	4.75×10^{-4}	2.07
320	0.0048	1.03	1.16×10^{-4}	2.04

Table 4.7: L^1-errors for the 1D non-convex HJ problem (4.4) before the singularity formation. $T = 0.8/\pi^2$.

N	First-order method		Second-order method	
	L^1-error	L^1-order	L^1-error	L^1-order
40	0.1057	–	0.0248	–
80	0.0515	1.04	6.92×10^{-3}	1.84
160	0.0248	1.05	1.89×10^{-3}	1.87
320	0.0121	1.04	4.96×10^{-4}	1.93

Table 4.8: L^1-errors for the 1D non-convex HJ problem (4.4) after the singularity formation. $T = 1.5/\pi^2$.

N	First-order method		Second-order method	
	L^1-error	L^1-order	L^1-error	L^1-order
50	0.4046612	–	0.0402387	–
100	0.195242	1.05	0.00999105	2.01
200	0.0958819	1.03	0.0024644	2.02

Table 4.9: L^1-errors for the 2D non-convex HJ problem (4.5) before the singularity formation. $T = 0.8/\pi^2$.

N	First-order method		Second-order method	
	L^1-error	L^1-order	L^1-error	L^1-order
50	0.705644	–	0.0837231	–
100	0.334981	1.07	0.0215121	1.96
200	0.161502	1.05	0.00555327	1.95

Table 4.10: L^1-errors for the 2D non-convex HJ problem (4.5) after the singularity formation. $T = 1.5/\pi^2$.

and second-order 2D schemes before and after the singularity formation are given in Tables 4.9–4.10 and confirm the expected order of accuracy of our methods.

The extension of (4.5) to 3D reads

$$\phi_t - \cos(\phi_x + \phi_y + \phi_z + 1) = 0, \tag{4.6}$$

The initial data is taken as $\phi(x, y, 0) = -\cos(\pi(x + y + z)/3)$. The convergence rates for the first- and second-order 3D schemes are given in Tables 4.11–4.12.

N	First-order method		Second-order method	
	L^1-error	L^1-order	L^1-error	L^1-order
50	5.071	–	0.603	–
100	2.55	0.99	0.150	2.01
200	1.142	1.16	0.035	2.10

Table 4.11: L^1-errors for the 3D non-convex HJ problem (4.6) before the singularity formation. $T = 0.08$.

N	First-order method		Second-order method	
	L^1-error	L^1-order	L^1-error	L^1-order
50	8.594	–	1.100	–
100	4.26	1.01	0.299	1.88
200	1.913	1.16	0.075	1.99

Table 4.12: L^1-errors for the 3D non-convex HJ problem (4.6) after the singularity formation. $T = 0.152$.

Example 3: A linear advection equation

In this example we solve the 1D linear advection equation, i.e., the Hamiltonian is taken as $H(\phi_x) = \phi_x$. We assume periodic boundary conditions on $[-1, 1]$, and take the initial data as $\phi(x, 0) = g(x - 0.5)$ on $[-1, 1]$, where

$$g(x) = -\left(\frac{\sqrt{3}}{2} + \frac{9}{2} + \frac{2\pi}{3}\right)(x + 1) + h(x),$$

$$h(x) = \begin{cases} 2\cos\left(\frac{3\pi}{2}x^2\right) - \sqrt{3}, & -1 < x < -\frac{1}{3}, \\ \frac{3}{2} + 3\cos(2\pi x), & -\frac{1}{3} < x < 0, \\ \frac{15}{2} - 3\cos(2\pi x), & 0 < x < \frac{1}{3}, \\ \frac{1}{3}(28 + 4\pi + \cos(3\pi x)) - \frac{8\pi}{3\sqrt{3}}\cos\left(\frac{\pi}{2}x\right), & \frac{1}{3} < x < 1. \end{cases}$$

This example was designed as to be similar to the one used in [12]. An error in that reference prevents us from repeating it exactly. The results of the second-order method are shown in Figure 4.9. The dissipation effects are visible in the round-off of the corners.

Example 4: 2D eikonal equation in geometric optics

We demonstrate the results obtained with the 2D scheme on the non-convex problem

$$\begin{cases} \phi_t + \sqrt{\phi_x^2 + \phi_y^2 + 1} = 0, \\ \phi(x, y, 0) = \frac{1}{4}(\cos(2\pi x) - 1)(\cos(2\pi y) - 1) - 1. \end{cases} \tag{4.7}$$

This model arises in geometric optics [15]. The results of our second-order method at time $T = 0.6$ are shown in Figure 4.10, where we see the sharp corners that develop in this problem, in agreement with the results in [30].

Example 5: Optimal control

We solve a 2D problem with a more general Hamiltonian of the form $H(x, y, \nabla\phi)$. This is an optimal control problem related to cost determination [33].

$$\begin{cases} \phi_t - \sin(y)\phi_x + \sin(x)\phi_y + |\phi_y| - \frac{1}{2}\sin^2(y) - 1 + \cos(x) = 0, \\ \phi(x, y, 0) = 0. \end{cases} \tag{4.8}$$

This example develops a complex singularity structure. The result of our second-order scheme is in qualitative agreement with [30] as can be seen in Figure 4.11.

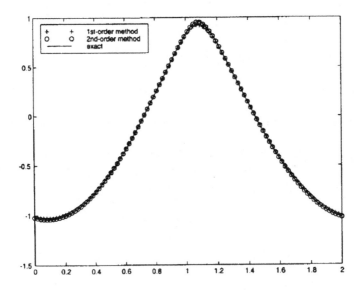

Figure 4.1: *Example 1*. The 1D convex Hamiltonian (4.1) before the formation of singularities. $T = 0.8/\pi^2$. $N = 100$. Shown are the first-order approximation, the second-order approximation and the exact solution.

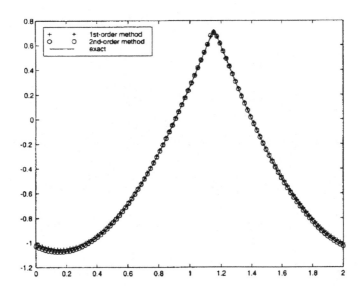

Figure 4.2: *Example 1.* The 1D convex Hamiltonian (4.1) after the formation of singularities. $T = 1.5/\pi^2$. $N = 100$. Shown are the first-order approximation, the second-order approximation and the exact solution.

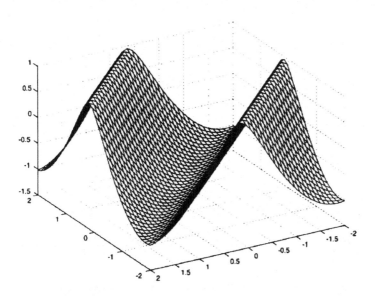

Figure 4.3: *Example 1.* The 2D convex Hamiltonian (4.2) before the formation of singularities. $T = 0.8/\pi^2$. $N = 40 \times 40$.

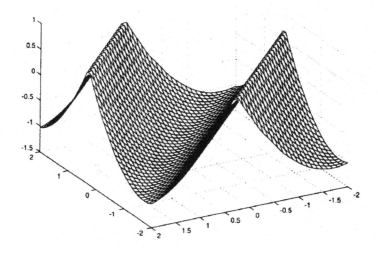

Figure 4.4: *Example 1.* The 2D convex Hamiltonian (4.2) after the formation of singularities. $T = 1.5/\pi^2$. $N = 40 \times 40$.

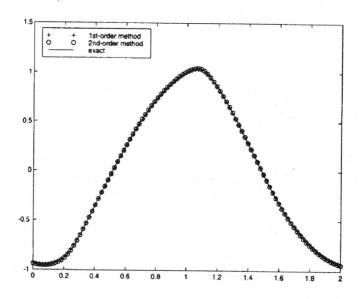

Figure 4.5: *Example 2.* The 1D non-convex Hamiltonian (4.4) before the formation of singularities. $T = 0.8/\pi^2$. $N = 100$. Shown are the first-order approximation, the second-order approximation and the exact solution.

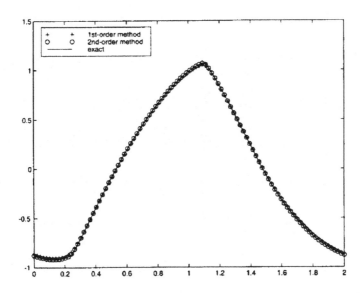

Figure 4.6: *Example 2.* The 1D non-convex Hamiltonian (4.4) after the formation of singularities. $T = 1.5/\pi^2$. $N = 100$. Shown are the first-order approximation, the second-order approximation and the exact solution.

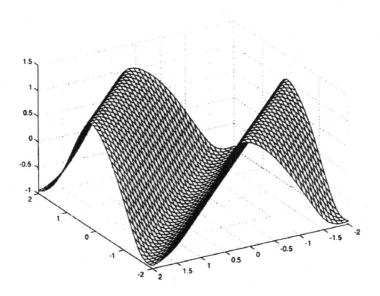

Figure 4.7: *Example 2.* The 2D non-convex Hamiltonian (4.2) before the formation of singularities. $T = 0.8/\pi^2$. $N = 40 \times 40$.

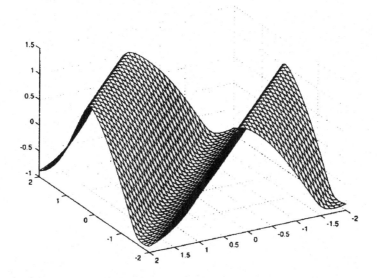

Figure 4.8: *Example 2.* The 2D non-convex Hamiltonian (4.2) after the formation of singularities. $T = 1.5/\pi^2$. $N = 40 \times 40$.

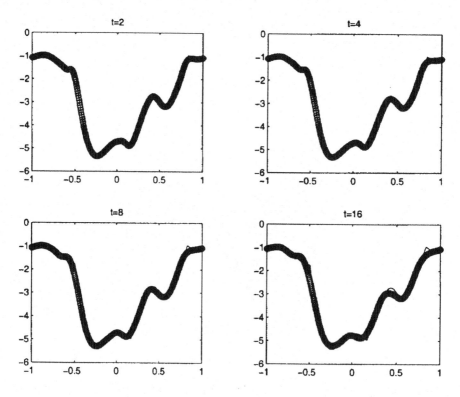

Figure 4.9: *Example 3.* A 1D linear advection problem. $N = 400$.

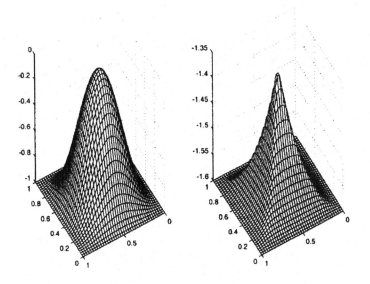

Figure 4.10: *Example 4*. The 2D eikonal equation (4.7). $N = 40 \times 40$. Left: the initial data. Right: the solution at $T = 0.6$.

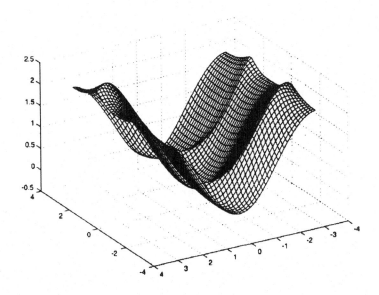

Figure 4.11: *Example 5*. The 2D optimal control problem (4.8). $T = 1$. $N = 40 \times 40$.

Appendix A: A Second-Order 2D MATLAB Implementation

We present an example of a MATLAB implementation of Algorithm 3.1 in 2D. The following code provides the core computations for a single time step, but does not include any handling of boundary conditions. The functions H(phix, phiy), Hphix(phix, phiy) and Hphiy(phix, phiy) return, respectively, the Hamiltonian $H(\varphi_x, \varphi_y)$ and the derivatives of the Hamiltonian $\frac{\partial H(\varphi_x, \varphi_y)}{\partial \varphi_x}$ and $\frac{\partial H(\varphi_x, \varphi_y)}{\partial \varphi_y}$. The function minmod is the slope limiter defined in Section 2.2. This code is somewhat optimized for speed at the expense of storage, and $h := \Delta x$, $k := \Delta t$.

```
a1 = 1/(2 + sqrt(2));
a2 = a1*(a1-1)/2;
a3 = a1*a1/2;
a4 = (2*a1-1)/2;
a5 = a1/2;
h2 = h*h;
twoh2 = 2*h2;
kover2 = k/2;
for i=1:N
    for j=1:N % compute the first differences
        dphix(i,j) = phi(i+1,j) - phi(i,j);
        dphiy(i,j) = phi(i,j+1) - phi(i,j);
    end
end
for i=1:N
    im = i-1;
    ip = i+1;
    for j=1:N % compute the limited second differences
        jm = j-1;
        jp = j+1;
        dphixx(i,j) = minmod(dphix(ip,j) - dphix(i,j), dphix(ip,j) - dphix(im,j), dphix(i,j) - dphix(im,j));
        dphiyx(i,j) = minmod(dphiy(ip,j) - dphiy(i,j), dphiy(ip,j) - dphiy(im,j), dphiy(i,j) - dphiy(im,j));
        dphixy(i,j) = minmod(dphix(i,jp) - dphix(i,j), dphix(i,jp) - dphix(i,jm), dphix(i,j) - dphix(i,jm));
        dphiyy(i,j) = minmod(dphiy(i,jp) - dphiy(i,j), dphiy(i,jp) - dphiy(i,jm), dphiy(i,j) - dphiy(i,jm));
    end
end
for i=1:N
    for j=1:N
        im = i-1;
        jm = j-1;
        dphixyp = dphiyx(i,j) + dphixy(i,j);
        dphixym = dphiyx(i,jm) + dphixy(im,j);
        phip = phi(i,j) + a1*(dphix(i,j) + dphiy(i,j)) + a2*(dphixx(i,j) + dphiyy(i,j)) + a3*dphixyp;
```

```
        phim = phi(i,j) - a1*(dphix(im,j) + dphiy(i,jm)) + a2*(dphixx(im,j) + dphiyy(i,jm)) + a3*dphixym;

        phixp = (dphix(i,j) + a4*dphixx(i,j) + a5*dphixyp)/h;

        phiyp = (dphiy(i,j) + a4*dphiyy(i,j) + a5*dphixyp)/h;

        phixm = (dphix(im,j) - a4*dphixx(im,j) - a5*dphixym)/h;

        phiym = (dphiy(i,jm) - a4*dphiyy(i,jm) - a5*dphixym)/h;

        phixtp = -Hphix(phixp, phiyp)*dphixx(i,j)/h2 - Hphiy(phixp, phiyp)*dphixyp/twoh2;

        phiytp = -Hphix(phixp, phiyp)*dphixyp/twoh2 - Hphiy(phixp, phiyp)*dphiyy(i,j)/h2;

        phixtm = -Hphix(phixm, phiym)*dphixx(im,j)/h2 - Hphiy(phixm, phiym)*dphixym/twoh2;

        phiytm = -Hphix(phixm, phiym)*dphixym/twoh2 - Hphiy(phixm, phiym)*dphiyy(i,jm)/h2;

        phihatp(i,j) = phip - k*H(phixp + kover2*phixtp, phiyp + kover2*phiytp);

        phihatm(i,j) = phim - k*H(phixm + kover2*phixtm, phiym + kover2*phiytm);

    end

end

Dp = (1-2*a1)*h*sqrt(2);

Dm = Dp;

D2 = (D0 + Dp)/2;

D0o8D2 = D0*D0/(8*D2);

for i=1:N

    for j=1:N

        ip = i+1;

        jp = j+1;

        im = i-1;

        jm = j-1;

        dphi0 = (phihatp(i,j) - phihatm(i,j))/D0;

        dphip = (phihatm(ip,jp) - phihatp(i,j))/Dp;

        dphim = (phihatm(i,j) - phihatp(im,jm))/Dm;

        d2phi = minmod(dphip - dphi0, dphip - dphim, dphi0 - dphim);

        phi(i,j) = (phihatp(i,j) + phihatm(i,j))/2 - D0o8D2*d2phi;

    end

end
```

References

[1] Abgrall R., *Numerical discretization of the first-order Hamilton-Jacobi equation on triangular meshes*, Comm. Pure Appl. Math., **49**, (1996), pp.1339–1373.

[2] Arminjon P., Viallon M.-C., *Généralisation du Schéma de Nessyahu-Tadmor pour Une Équation Hyperbolique à Deux Dimensions D'espace*, C.R. Acad. Sci. Paris, **t. 320** , série I. (1995), pp.85–88.

[3] Barles G., *Solution de viscosité des équations de Hamilton-Jacobi*, Springer-Verlag, Berlin, 1994.

[4] Bianco F., Puppo G., Russo G., *High order central schemes for hyperbolic systems of conservation laws*, SIAM J. Sci. Comp., **21**, (1999), pp.294–322.

[5] Crandall M.G., Evans L.C., Lions P.-L., *Some properties of viscosity solutions of Hamilton-Jacobi equations*, Trans. Amer. Math. Soc., **282**, (1984), pp.487–502.

[6] Crandall M.G., Ishii H., Lions P.-L., *User's guide to viscosity solutions of second order partial differential equations*, Bull. Amer. Math. Soc., **27**, (1992), pp.1-67.

[7] Crandall M.G., Lions P.-L., *Viscosity solutions of Hamilton-Jacobi equations*, Trans. Amer. Math. Soc., **277** (1983), pp.1–42.

[8] Crandall M.G., Lions P.-L., *Two approximations of solutions of Hamilton-Jacobi equations*, Math. Comp., **43**, (1984), pp.1–19.

[9] Friedrichs K. O., Lax P. D., *Systems of conservation equations with a convex extension*, Proc. Nat. Acad. Sci., **68**, (1971), pp.1686–1688.

[10] Hu C., Shu C.-W., *A discontinuous Galerkin finite element method for Hamilton-Jacobi equations*, SIAM J. Sci. Comp., **21**, (1999), pp.666–690.

[11] Kruzkov S.N., *The Cauchy problem in the large for nonlinear equations and for certain quasilinear systems of the first order with several variables*, Soviet Math. Dokl., **5**, (1964), pp.493–496.

[12] Jiang G.-S., Peng D., *Weighted ENO schemes for Hamilton-Jacobi equations*, SIAM J. Sci. Comp., **21**, (2000), pp.2126–2143.

[13] Jiang G.-S., Shu C.-W., *Efficient implementation of weighted ENO schemes*, JCP, **126**, (1996), pp.202–228.

[14] Jiang G.-S., Tadmor E., *Nonoscillatory central schemes for multidimensional hyperbolic conservation laws*, SIAM J. Sci. Comp., **19**, (1998), pp.1892–1917.

[15] Jin S., Xin Z., *Numerical passage from systems of conservation laws to Hamilton-Jacobi equations and relaxation schemes*, SIAM J. Numer. Anal., **35**, (1998), pp.2385–2404.

[16] Kurganov A., Levy D., *A third-order semi-discrete scheme for conservation laws and convection-diffusion equations*, SIAM J. Sci. Comp., **22**, (2000), pp.1461–1488

[17] Kurganov A., Noelle S., Petrova G., *Semi-discrete central-upwind schemes for hyperbolic conservation laws and Hamilton-Jacobi equations*, SIAM J. Sci. Comp., to appear.

[18] Kurganov A., Tadmor E., *New high-resolution semi-discrete central schemes for Hamilton-Jacobi equations*, JCP, **160**, (2000), pp.720–724.

[19] Kurganov A., Tadmor E., *New high-resolution central schemes for nonlinear conservation laws and convection-diffusion equations*, JCP, **160**, (2000), pp.241–282.

[20] Lax P. D., *Weak solutions of non-linear hyperbolic equations and their numerical computation*, CPAM, **7**, (1954), pp.159–193.

[21] van Leer B., *Towards the ultimate conservative difference scheme, V. A second-order sequel to Godunov's method*, JCP, **32**, (1979), pp.101–136.

[22] Lepsky O., Hu C., Shu C.-W., *Analysis of the discontinuous Galerkin method for Hamilton-Jacobi equations*, Appl. Numer. Math., **33**, (2000), pp.423–434.

[23] Levy D., Puppo G., Russo G., *Central WENO schemes for hyperbolic systems of conservation laws*, Math. Model. and Numer. Anal., **33**, no. 3 (1999), pp.547–571.

[24] Levy D., Puppo G., Russo G., *Compact central WENO schemes for multidimensional conservation laws*, SIAM J. Sci. Comp., **22**, (2000), pp.656–672.

[25] Lions P.L., *Generalized solutions of Hamilton-Jacobi equations*, Pitman, London, 1982.

[26] Lions P.L., Souganidis P.E., *Convergence of MUSCL and filtered schemes for scalar conservation laws and Hamilton-Jacobi equations*, Numer. Math., **69**, (1995), pp.441–470.

[27] Liu X.-D., Osher S., *Nonoscillatory high order accurate self-similar maximum principle satisfying shock capturing schemes I*, SIAM J. Numer. Anal., **33**, no. 2 (1996), pp.760–779.

[28] Liu X.-D., Tadmor E., *Third order nonoscillatory central scheme for hyperbolic conservation laws*, Numer. Math., **79**, (1998), pp.397–425.

[29] Lin C.-T., Tadmor E., L^1-*stability and error estimates for approximate Hamilton-Jacobi solutions*, Numer. Math., **87**, (2001), pp.701–735.

[30] Lin C.-T., Tadmor E., *High-resolution non-oscillatory central schemes for approximate Hamilton-Jacobi equations*, SIAM J. Sci. Comp., **21**, no. 6, (2000), pp.2163–2186.

[31] Nessyahu H., Tadmor E., *Non-oscillatory central differencing for hyperbolic conservation laws*, JCP, **87**, no. 2 (1990), pp.408–463.

[32] Osher S., Sethian J., *Fronts propagating with curvature dependent speed: algorithms based on Hamilton-Jacobi formulations*, JCP, **79**, (1988), pp.12–49.

[33] Osher S., Shu C.-W., *High-order essentially nonoscillatory schemes for Hamilton-Jacobi equations*, SIAM J. Numer. Anal., **28**, (1991), pp.907–922.

[34] Shu C.-W., *Essentially non-oscillatory and weighted essentially non-oscillatory schemes for hyperbolic conservation laws* in Advanced Numerical Approximation of Nonlinear Hyperbolic Equations, Lecture Notes in Mathematics (editor: A. Quarteroni), Springer, Berlin, 1998.

[35] Shu C.-W., Osher S., *Efficient implementation of essentially non-oscillatory shock-capturing schemes, II*, JCP, **83**, (1989), pp.32–78.

[36] Souganidis P.E., *Approximation schemes for viscosity solutions of Hamilton-Jacobi equations*, J. Diff. Equations., **59**, (1985), pp.1–43.

[37] Sweby P.K., *High-resolution schemes using flux limiters for hyperbolic conservation laws*, SIAM J. Numer. Anal., **21**, (1984), pp.995–1011.

CPSIA information can be obtained at www.ICGtesting.com
Printed in the USA
BVOW09s1017180215

388285BV00015B/141/P